REVERIES OF LONGING

REVERIES OF LONGING

Melissa Kiguwa

African perspectives

·P U B L I S H I N G·

www.africanperspectives.co.za

www.africanperspectives.co.za

African Perspectives Publishing
P.O. Box 9342
Grant Park 2051
Johannesburg,
South Africa
E mail: francis@africanperspectives.co.za
Website: www.africanperspectives.co.za
Facebook: African Perspectives Publishing

Cover artist: Olga Lolo

ISBN: 978-0-9922285-3-8

CONTENTS

CONTENTS

Author's Note

I used to love the parable of the reckless son who leaves his father's wealthy home for the thrill and glamor of the city. In place of the adventure he searches for, he finds utter desolation.

No thrill. No glamor.

In fact, he eats worse than the pigs at his father's home. The story ends when the son, finally aware of his mistake, returns home and finds a celebratory party to welcome him home. Pigs are slaughtered, wine is ever-flowing – the prodigal son who was once lost is now found.

It would be years before I realized prodigal children do not exist. There is no one waiting on the other side with expectant arms.

Code-switched tongues are heard with suspicion: these tongues both exotic and foreign to those they call their people, their family.

And so, children of migration, displacement, revolution, and diaspora makeshift "home" in dilapidated welfare housing complexes, desert land before borders, in slums, on barrio street corners, and inside camps for refugees and internally displaced persons. These same children look for acceptance in cultural enclaves in the city, in sex, in love, in faith- based communities and shrines, and in majik.

Catharsis in exodus

My prayer is simple: as empire-building shifts and grows, may we who are caught in the crosswires create brave ways of imagining ourselves. May we have the strength to tell our own stories. May we speak in solidarity with each other, to each other. May we love unabashedly and fearlessly. And may we find (or create) for ourselves safety, peace, and home.

"You said, 'I will go to another land, I will go to another sea.
Another city will be found, better than this...'

New lands you will not find, you will not find other seas.
The city will follow you..."

[Constantine P. Cavafy, *The City*]

At a Womyn's Meeting in Phoenix

[*where there is a woman there is magic: ntozake shange*]

we

called ourselves the haphazard
abortion of our mothers'
dreams

even while we welcomed each other
in fornicated yoruba

poured sankofa catch ups in
black green and red teacups

we knew ourselves not quite
what we wanted to be

we climbed fore mothered mountains
in honor of lunar cycles

howled to the moon
in remembrance
of an estranged wildness

we would laugh
chanting our names into prayer beads
our liturgies the smell of
burning sage

and at night
we cried

ashamed the lives we lived
were those of our mothers

how we still picked men
who left like our fathers

Hometown Checkpoints

we met at the crux of
hometown checkpoints

the scar above your lip
crescent moon dipped
water giving life

i drank over and over
a fountain of bricks breaking
to the sound of automated
revolving hesitation

>　　*tell me habibti,*
>　　*when did the salt of my*
>　　*skin remind you*
>　　*of refugee camps*
>　　*turned backyard bars?*

your skin　honey blossomed apartheid
　　mine　barbed wire burnt mango

lips etched in exile

in bed we both carried
blown twin towers in the
womb of our memory

you said
　　　modernity is to the arab
　　　as commerce is to the african

i said
　　　if there is difference between us,
　　　it is in passports detained and visa numbers

we held this unholy carnage
left to saunter atop sky
scraping progress

and now you are gone

so far away from here

  so far away from me

Reflections in the City: I

was i not here before

pieces of myself left in barefaced
water bodies\ the wailing
narratives from the bottom of atlantic oceans

i chose the journey of troubadour

wrapped myself in nomad only to
name\ then rename me lonely\ flailing constantly\
consistently into the unfamiliar

you see there are more ways to fall between the
cracks\ of nothingness and failure

so i fling myself upon any sail\ curly
headed or fermented and malted\

as long as its winds carry me to the next port

Planting Season

where are you now?

there are red mogadishu
flowers in front of
the tarpaulin tent where she sleeps

blood of my blood
flesh of my flesh

she winds coarse black
tresses around the
stalks of her wrists

have you found it there?

hair of sons
she has not seen in
more than ten years

have you found it now?

strands removed from
head chin chest

and what of me?

any semblance
of sometime flesh

without
home
home
home

The Brooklyn Village Womyn

i tell her she can only run so long 'til cross country bridges give
way. tell her she musta mistaken herself for some west african
creole womyn washed up in the new orleans 9th ward

and she's confused.

learned to wrap stories around shoulders for protection. wound
pashmina memories from shoulder blade to shoulder blade
making sure neck to back covered. times is chilly   so she always
wants to be secured.

but this time   time was slow coming. a pang started from turn
styled bellies too used to usa packaged rice and too dry tasting
maize. she tries to cross stitch the pain away   rock herself in
another womyn's tender to childhood away adult girl memories.

see   she was born in a hospital to cold hands with no home
promised and it's fitting because she's been looking for home
ever since. she rests only when told but sleeps with her third eye
open. the other two close, but always in remembrance of what
crawls in the dark.

it doesn't always have to be biting roaches
or big scary men

for her it is the fear of demons who fly into pigs
and cause convulsions.

in the mornings
she mistakes disappearing acts for
the rapture until she realizes

everyone leaves some time or another.

she tells me

> *palm lines only tell you*
> *how far your river can reach*

> *but they never tell you why*
> *nobody wants to swim in your waters,*

> *never tell you where the fishes went or why*
> *fresh water springs turn to swampy hollowed caves*

i tell her   no amount of chewed miraa and smoked emindi takes the pain away. she tells me the story of a man who has a wound that won't heal. five years his wound still pusses because something pierced him that shouldn't. she says   maybe he and her are cosmic soul mates   his leg   her heart.

i tell her   life wasn't made for all of us. maybe she's like vanilla in a desert or a baby in an internment camp

not meant to survive   at all.

she tells me   maybe at some point in time she was supposed to sing universal lullabies and maybe the sun really does shine in her eyes   but those are talents for the blessed of the earth. and she   carrying the weight of babylonian towers and civilized promises   can't afford to sing right now.

she has a heart that won't stop pussing and eyes that won't stay open.

Lonely to Destitute

jazz
persian
cracked
concrete
songs
of
wine

while drunk sailors float
against lapping waves
of sand turned oceans

weep for the chilean
hummingbird trapped inside
reveries of longing

belly into the whirlpool
of candid silhouettes that
have become your
hollowed cheeks

wail your
love
lost,
a
farsi
metaphored
melody.

Dating 101

don't talk geopolitical borders on the first date. don't show
yourself night dancing with harriet along the modern day
underground railroad. how you read tolstoy and ngũgĩ in one
week drawing lines from kenya to russia back to sense. leave out
loves lost. draw yourself strong. an anthem. pied piper history.
show depth. pay for the meal. leave behind nothing but strewn
charismatic deceit. alone, rock yourself to sleep.

Insurgent Love-Making

<u>a call:</u>

kiss to freeze time,

press mouth to mouth as
though survival,

clit to clit whet
like separated chaff
on the threshing room floor,

bless her face with
sticky remembrances.

<u>interlude:</u>

men you wish you could love

if only you had not traversed the dusty
road to gomorrah.

<u>a response:</u>

i, too, used to be ashamed of this love,

until i tasted the veil tear between
your legs,

circled your ka'bah
seven times, more times

counterclockwise until i
touched the strength inside your voice.

i never knew power
until i saw you speak.

never knew divinity until
i saw you rebuild babel
bloody snatch by bloody snatch

only to
ask the heavens
if they missed you.

Wanderlust

these
  hands
    crave
      slow
        trailings

          explore
            each salty grain
              as though
                topographer

                  bypass lineages
                of past names
              until every
            valley along these
sinewy maps

litanies
  you
    how
      far
        i
          travelled
        to
      be
here

Brimstone in the Promised Land

in boston, wrinkled brown women

remember their mothers' villages
on drying clothes pinned atop welfare balconies,

while televisions play
reruns of *the price is right*,

old white women's homes gleam
like pennies sent back home.

> *the daughters of these wrinkled brown women*
> *corner-stitch rituals to salve the splice*
> *that has become their mother's tongue*

in boston, mothers marry
american men for green cards,

they attend church in school buildings
where cadillac toothed pastors

speak in building fund tithes.

> *pray to obatala and mukasa*
> *wear kitenge cooking fufu*

three years long, wrinkled brown women tithe,

praying to give their daughters everything
they never had.

these mothers bridge continents
through darkened nipples

> *they cry themselves to sleep*
> *wondering why amerikkka did not keep its*
> *promise*

Church Politics

the good brown girls sit
in front pews
with big handkerchiefs placed
delicately on their laps

their fingers
olive branches glorying
delilah in esther's voice

their mothers sing
exaltation in vibrato

birthing redemption
for those sitting in the
  back pew

Reflections in the City: II

he reminds me only jesus
knows the heavy cross we carry, only
jesus can love our withered hands.

he told my mother
he would never touch a child
born out of wedlock.

singing hymns on the phone,
he asks if my faith is pure now,

i want to kiss his withered hands.

filled with the realization even the most heathen
child needs to be cradled by rooted fingers,

he held me.

Butch Queens at a Funeral

it is named an abomination

what these words do to
  moist wet holes

how they find ways to penetrate

        under mosquito nets
    in   between bible
thumping aunties

name it something else

amidst funeral rites
  thighs whisper touched
    by mourning boys

with sleepy eyelids that sip
from gourd shaped asses

  name it an insurgency
subversive radical fucking

watch how their hands switch
  like hips grinding air

with
    pink dotted   tongues as
 sustenance

name it sanctified,
  the way they wash each other anew

Raise the Sun

there are mud packed huts hidden
between the crevice of your elbows,

moon shaped daggers sequined under
the curve of your fingernails.

with monsoons inside your voice,
an avalanche inside your belly,

you raise the sun like hallelujah.

Nobody Talks

nobody talks about the way losing a love\
does more\ than ache your heart

it presses into lungs\ chokes
blood flow\ tracks artery lines
like bridge wires

until all in all is falling down

sometimes\ you feel the tear

cartilage shredding\ fat
shearing\ ligaments twisting\
muscles ripping

nobody talks\ about black hearts holding onto other
black\ brown\ beating hearts

a serial hunter\ this ache

nobody sings/ the way this ache be
a travellin' kinda wound

As if the Gods were Playing

IV

when he,

carrying earthquakes
in pocket,

the first revolution
balled in fists,

first landed in uganda, he
kissed the ground.

I

which previous dusk forecasted this?

VI

another man,

carrying refugee melodies via palestine,

plans to enter jerusalem
for the first time.

II

there are freedom songs sung from haiti via uganda
via palestine.

this is today.

VIII

israeli immigration denies him holy land entrance.

III

unrequited love:
   the space of your memory filled with oil-detonated contracts.

V

it was an unrequited love:

   him burning the songs of a thousand moon stones,
   this africa folding out of itself.

VII

singing, *bismillah allahu akbar*

his heart tap dances the right to movement
for his daughter~

i promised you this:
this freedom, this home, this is what
   god looks like.

A Poet's Prayer

belly into me

remind me i am more than
                  resistance and survival

weather me beautiful

save me from forlorn promises left
               on the front of my verandah

               with hands that cup faith like rain

banish me back into me
               into you

Afro-Wanderings

maybe it was the *crik crak*
of too many tumbling talismans.

too busy dancing in the midst of
 ra-ra drum circles and spiked berry-berry sherbet,

maybe it was majik.

two-step toned bass turned you into eshu.

>keep weaving,

>remind me of these nonstop foot to
>pavement poundings,

>take back morning bouts of nostalgia,
>stale coffee, awkward sex,

>snort these circles of *crak*,

just enough to reach
between here and back.

>stop pulsating,

>remember there was a time
>we roamed together,

crik crak to that.

On Distance

they say
absence makes
the heart grow fonder

i don't know who they is
but they don't know

this distance
this absence

Sense

i want
 to make
sense
    of you.

make
 sense
    to you.

  make time
 consuming
sense
  with
you.

M

you are from the north,
so i tongue travel
   earlobe to neck cradle

retracing your journey from
ancestral village to my bed.

in one night i learn
the contours of your face

your eyes like your hellos
i never know if what you say
is what you mean.

but your cheeks speak
words familiar

so i kiss

over and over, until i
realize

holding onto the back of your head is not enough.

i want to devour you.

sink feeling into
warm wetness,

falling slowly into
the salvation of your face,

i taste what could be
on your tongue.

I Speak a Holy Ghost

i speak a holy ghost when i see one
   vibrate /sound \to magic/ to chest\

i speak rainwater baptismal noise
   calabash black static in drip drops

   poured mouth to mouth
      i hear you   speaking \backhanded/ political plays
                     in corner store alleyways

you speak \broken back/ mama tears
   \sun drunk horus/ clouds

we speak sound like isis
   \ankh flavored goddess/ of the month

we speak god

Reflections in the City: III

his eyes aglow with the
knowledge of the redeemed,

mine closed in remembrance of
sore kneecaps bent to pray for wishes
that never came true;

my grandfather tells me to stop
making elixirs out of dreams.

i want to tell him i can't walk on water.

never heard of anybody that could
except for his savior,

but i don't pray to him either.

mostly i want to ask,
weren't you thunderous hurricanes once?
an emotional whirlwind from womb to boom

your extravagance measured by
a little of this but not too much of that because
it's hard when you're nothing you were meant to be.

i know.

you could have been
sanskrit praying,
ramadan fasting,
ma'at priesting,
but here you are,

waiting.

prayers are like whispers to the wind,

maybe the divine hears but
you'd do more as a radioactive cell
in the middle of the ocean.

nuclear never felt so hallowed until it erupted.

but we never say words
that are most honest,

simply allow dust to gather
around syllables caught between the
hymn in our throat.

Forced Penetration

in to congo
out of tuskegee

in to somalia
out of vietnam

in to afghanistan

If I were to Blow up the Embassy

if i were to blow up the embassy it would be calculated

pink skin bare bone specific

explosive

sticks of dynamite

stuck so far up my ass

you'd call it
integrated diplomacy

if i were to blow up the embassy it would be calculated

the aftermath featuring confused

interviewees calling me

the sweet organized intern

who led workshops on cross cultural democracy

my fragile existence

expounded by a heart woven mother

only a bomb's distance away

if i were to blow up the embassy it would be calculated

an ultrasonic   *boom*

                    and if i stood before the glory of god

            when the deed was done

my charred feet would be the

                    gnosis of an immaculate submission of will

3:43 a.m.

location: guantanamo/ jerusalem/ u.s.-mexico border

four bowed heads
praying
to a god
that had
forsaken them

long before a migrant mother
strapped an un-chosen child to her chest
like explosives in the market,

long before she roamed parched wasteland
dreaming the dreams of

sand skeletons,
of roaming vultures.

four bowed heads:

raúl
carlos
jesús
omar

or was it

omar
mohammed
amir
abdullah

why did god forsake
these four men with bowed heads?

blindfolded by burlap
one whispers liturgies
into the darkness:

padre, perdónalos porque no
saben lo que hacen

3:43 a.m.
or
1:43 p.m.?

take back every moment of every second
to hear the gun shells blasting,

picture pink mist frozen in the
never-land of their prayers.

a woman
buys bread
1:42 in the afternoon.

at 1:43
hagar enters the market
with explosives strapped to
her chest like an un-chosen child
in the desert,

and in these
parts, which are all
parts, all that was,
that is, that comes

explodes.

To Trayvon and Oscar and Emmitt and Him and Him and Him and Him

trayvon,
are you there?

i started this poem for you
not knowing it would be a prayer to you

oscar,
were you there?
when the gavel cracked
did it sound like what was done to your back?

emmitt,
can you forgive us here?

still planting seeds of color
unlike the rose out of concrete
we stay stuck to the repeat

oscar,
are you there?

trayvon,
do you hear me?

i started this poem for you
not knowing it would be a prayer to you

they say god don't like ugly
is that why she took you–
needed to take away from this place
that can't see how beautiful you really are?

Reflections in the City: IV

i am looking for the holy.
the beautiful.

the rhythms between the spaces in these words.
the ghosts mirroring the words i never say.
the words i never had the courage to speak.
the courage to speak them.

the words:
holy,
beautiful,
courageous.

Lust

her naked body
   is uncharted terrain

   goose pimpled skin
   adorning lithe arches

   a sienna burnt passageway
   stretched past the plains of pangea

Take Over

splayed soft lips

in front of you
deliciously open

so un-imperial

you always ask before
taking me over

How to Love a Revolutionary

I

the first time i showed you my
wounds,

you pretended you couldn't smell the ash
suppurating from the opening in my
skin.

as if lips parted resurrect
burnt temples,

you tried to messiah
into me.

II

most nights,
we make love in a

darkness that sighs like creaky shoes –

using our bodies as hazy deserts
we camel drink slowly.

III

in the morning,
i wake up with juaréz on the brain.

IV

while baby girls draped in beads cling
red ochred mothers to their dusty backs,

three-foot-three children grow
stunted oaks in
the middle of caged cities.

V

boys become trees without the
luxury of knowing their strength,

arms of bare trunk bones,
limbs stripped fiber,
hearts planted bulbs.

VI

busy sewing scars with words, yet
mine keeps discharging.

VII

here you are, covered in
ash with no intention
of phoenixing out my bed.

VIII

the first time i showed you my wounds
you told me you knew how to leave this empire.

IX

we leave knowing

it has never been about
me and you.

Praise

we make love
like praise and worship

pray for manna but god
misheard our prayers

so splayed shrapnel rains

over syria
depending on the day.

Yoga PTSD

we stretch in ones and twos

lost click-clacked shackles
but still can't

twirl wrists the way
i need to

chattled in ones and twos

tip of finger
to tip of nose there are no
poses to release this

     breathe in

breathing,
body memory intact,
all else system down

     release

i am releasing

     breathe in

i am breathing

     release

breaking/ broken
   i am broken

Un-Broken

splinter me
   cracked shelf
   half life silent

peel me raw

husk by husk
   remember me
   beautiful

reach from
   crevice to hinge

palm me
   soft oil

rust stain me anew

splinter me
   post apocalyptic
   sojourner

nomad from
   flight to sight

follow me
   breathless
   bated

   moving confines of
   borders imprinted
   across lips

see me
   broken

watch how i rise

Acknowledgements

Mom and Dad the wordsmith in me always fails to find the words to say how deep, how loving, how amazing your energy, support, and encouragement has been. I am thankful for the both of you and everything you are. You allow me to bask in your glow while reminding me to shine on my own. Thank you, thank you, thank you.

A special thanks to Rose Francis and Mindy Stanford. Your belief in the "legs" of *Reveries of Longing* is cherished.

Monique Nettleford-Bruce, La Monica Everett, Ghazal Ghazi, Betty Kituyi, Raúl Al-qaraz Ochoa, Moses Serubiri, Luz Argueta-Vogel: your insight has made this book what it is. Your questions: tugging, pulling, interrogating. Together we asked ourselves: what does it all mean? You are appreciated and loved, thank you.

Those who may not have read the works during the process but have been involved in the conversations, your perspectives helped shape this book: Lady Godiva Akullo, Grace Atuhaire, Lytasha Blackwell, Olisadera Destiny Chukwu, Dustin Cox, Antoine Gary, Adam Geary, Mama Halima, Carmen Hernandez, Jennifer Hoefle, Sharmelle Hunte, Lesle Jansen, Maria Lopez, Peace Kiguwa, Marie-Laure Kamatali, Timothy Laku, Lori Lechien, Hannah Lozon, Stephanie Mach, Sheila Nanjego Marshall, Ambre Martino, Matt Matera, Darnell Moore, Maria Moore, Mohammed Naser, Julius Ntabanganya, Stella Nyanzi, Esa Rayyan, Christina Rigaud, Margarita Villa, and Ivy Zipporah. There are others I may not have listed by name but whose voices I carry with me.

And to the amazing foremothers and forefathers who have passed on in this physical realm but who have left legacies of poetic truth-telling, your brilliance carries me on.